# Missing

# Persons

*Stunning Cases Of Unsolved Missing People And Mysterious Missing Persons Cases: The True Stories*

Victor Ellanos

# Table of Contents

# Want more books?

Would you love books delivered straight to your inbox every week?

Free?

How about non-fiction books on all kinds of subjects?

We send out e-books to our loyal subscribers every week to download and enjoy!

All you have to do is join! It's so easy!

Just visit the link at the end of this book to sign up and then wait for your books to arrive!

# Introduction

Every missing person case is an agonizing experience. The anguish the family has to go through is unimaginable, at least. The life as they know it stops, and stays paused. The only time these people feel alive is when they hear news about their missing loved ones. The feeling of blood rushing to the head is not as comfortable as you would imagine. Not if you are awaiting bad news about someone you love.

Everyday, a lot of missing person reports are filed at police stations. Some of them include lost children-- some of them are missing adults. Some are purely by accident, while some have a touch of "malicious" intent as to why the disappearance happened.

In this book, we will have a detailed look at twelve people who have been living a normal life, until they were plucked out from it for unknown reasons. What their families have, up to now, are mere theories.

Some of them can already be considered dead, what with the amount years that passed without solid leads. For the cases that happened recently, their families are still hoping-- living by the belief that one day, they will be united.

Be prepared to work your mind on the possible scenarios...

Thanks again for purchasing this book, I hope you enjoy it!

# Chapter 1: **Percy Fawcett**

An archaeologist, a South American explorer and a British artillery officer, Lt. Colonel Percy Fawcett, disappeared along with his son in 1925 on an expedition to find a lost city called "Z". Though this city was nowhere found on any maps, he believed it existed. He was 58 years old when he went to that fateful expedition.

In 1925, Glove, a London-based financiers' group funded Fawcett for his exploratory expedition when he returned from Brazil along with one of his friends and Jack, his elder son. Having studied historical and legends records, he believed that there existed a lost city in the Mato Grosso region and he named that city, "Z".

Before leaving for this exploratory expedition, he left instructions for in case he failed to return. He wanted no rescue expedition to be sent for the fear that the rescuers would suffer because of his karma.

Percy had always been a perfectionist whenever he used to leave for an expedition. He never used to forget important necessities with him like powdered milk, canned foods, flares, guns, chronometer and a sextant. His elder son Jack and Jack's childhood friend, Raleigh Rimmell also accompanied Percy in his exploratory expedition.

He only chose two other companions with him for the expedition because he didn't want to risk getting caught by the native tribes as some of them could prove to be not so welcoming towards the explorers. Many of those tribes had not even met white men yet.

Percy, accompanied by his 2 companions, 2 Brazilian labourers, 8 mules, 2 horses and a pair of dogs left for his final expedition on 20th April, 1925. The last communication with him was made on 29th May, 1925 when he wrote a letter to his wife telling her that he was finally entering into the unexplored territory with only Rimmell and Jack.

The letter was delivered to his wife by a native runner. It was reported that they were crossing Upper Xingu which is a south-eastern tributary of the Amazon River. Their location was given by the final letter which was written from Dead horse camp and it was mostly optimistic.

With no further news or information coming after that, they were presumed to be killed by the local Indians because many tribes were near the same area at that time, namely, Kalapalos, Suyas, Arumas and Xavantes.

These were the tribes whose territories Percy and his companions were going to enter. Both of Percy's companions were ill when they were last seen. However, there is no proof of their murder. There are chances that they were probably killed by natural causes in the jungles of Brazil.

In the year 1927, a name plate of Percy was found with an Indian tribe. After that, in June 1933, a theodolite compass which belonged to Percy was found by Col. Aniceto Botelho close to Baciary Indians of the Mato Grosso. But, the nameplate which was found was from one of Percy's older expeditions and was probably gifted to the chief of the Indian tribe. The compass was found to have been left behind before entering the jungle of his last journey.

Many rescue expeditions were done in the following decades after that. But no sure results were found. There were many rumours and controversies circling around, but none of them could be verified. Other than the claim that Percy was probably killed by wild animals or the Indians, there were stories that claimed Percy had lost his memory and now was living as a leader of the cannibal's tribe.

About 100 rescuers were sent to uncover the fate of Fawcett. But nothing came out. One of the primitive expeditions was led by George Miller Dyott, an American explorer in the year 1927.

He claimed that he had found proof and clues of the death of Fawcett at the hands of Aloique Indian. But there were no specific evidence to his claims. An expedition done in the year 1951 unearthed some human bones but they were later found to be not connected to Fawcett or any of his companions.

Arne Falk-Ronne, a Danish explorer made a journey to Mato Grosso in the 1960s. In the year 1991, he wrote in a book that he learned about the fate of Percy from Orlando Villas- Boas, who had come in contact with one of the murderers of Fawcett. Seemingly, most of the gifts that Fawcett and his companion were carrying got lost in a mishap on the river.

To continue without the gifts was a serious law violation as per the rules of conduct. Because most of the members of the expedition were ill at that time, the Kalapalo tribe took the decision of killing them.

Jack and Raleigh's bodies were thrown into the river. Being an old man, the body of Colonel Fawcett was given a proper burial. Arne Falk Ronne visited the tribe and stated that one of the tribesmen gave the confirmation of Boas's story about why and how Percy was killed.

In the year 1951, an activist for the indigenous people, Orlando Villas- Boas allegedly found the bones of Percy and he got them analysed scientifically. The analysis apparently proved that they were Fauwcett's bones but Percy's younger son, Brian totally refused to accept it.

On this, Villas claimed that Brian didn't want to believe this because he was actually enjoying making money out of the books that were getting published and sold about his dad's disappearance. But it was later discovered that the bones that were found were not really Fawcett's after all. As of 1965, it was reported that the bones were resting in a box safely in a flat of the Villas brother in Sao Paulo.

In the year 1998, Benedict Allen, an English explorer went to talk to the Kalapalo Indians who were believed to have confessed the killing of the 3 Fawcett expedition members. Vajuvi though, the elder of the Kalapalo claimed in an interview by BBC that the bones which were found by Allen some 45 years ago were not Percy's bones. He also denied that his tribe was in anyway involved in the disappearance of the Fawcetts.

No definite clue supports any of the claims. And we still don't know where Percy's remain lie.

# Chapter 2: Amelia Earhart

The first ever female pilot who flew across the Atlantic Ocean, Amelia Earhart, disappeared when she was flying over the vast Pacific Ocean in the year 1937.

Born on 24th July, 1897, in the city of Atchison, Kansas, Amelia was dearly called as 'Lady Lindy'. She became the sixteenth woman to get a pilot's license in the year 1923. Not only this, she was the first woman to fly over the Atlantic Ocean in the year 1928.

She was also the first person to fly through both the Pacific Ocean and Atlantic Ocean. In the year 1937, she mysteriously disappeared when she was trying to fly along the equator. A number of theories about her last days have come up since then, out of which many have also been connected to some artefacts which were found in the Pacific Islands. These artefacts include tools, clothing and very recently, a freckle cream.

In the year 1935, Amelia joined Purdue University's faculty as a technical advisor and a career consultant in the Aeronautics department. This alliance helped her in financing the acquisition of a Lockheed Electra L-10E plane. Although, she was not the first person to navigate around the earth, she decided that she would fly along the circumference of the earth.

For that, she pulled together a top-rated crew of 3 men: Paul Mantz, who was a stunt pilot in Hollywood and was selected as Amelia's technical advisor; Fred Noonan, who had great experience in both flight as well as marine navigation and was selected as the 2nd navigator; and Captain Harry Manning, who had been President Roosevelt's Captain and was selected as Amelia's first navigator.

Their initial plan was to begin their journey from Oakland in California. From there they planned to fly towards the west to Hawaii. Then, they had decided to fly across the biggest ocean, the Pacific Ocean over to Australia. After that, their plan was to cross the sub-continents of India, Africa, and Florida and finally back to California.

They started their journey on the 17th March, 1937 from Oakland on the 1st leg. They had some periodic problems when they were flying over the Pacific and they landed in Hawaii to get some repairs done at the US Navy's field on the Ford Island in Pearl Harbour. Then after 3 days, they again took off, but something went wrong.

Amelia lost control and fuddled the plane on the track. It is still a controversy as to how this actually happened. Many witnesses said that they saw a tire blow. Among the witnesses was also the Associated Press Journalist.

Paul Mantz and some other sources indicated that it was the pilot's error. The good thing was that no-one was seriously hurt. But, the plane was badly broken and it had to be transferred back to California by ship for the purpose of thorough repairing.

Meanwhile, Putnam and Amelia secured extra funds for a new flight. The delay stress and the difficult fund-raising pretences made Earhart extremely tired. While the plane was being repaired, modifications were required to be made in the flight plan due to global wind changes and the change in weather patterns.

This time, Amelia and her crew decided to fly towards the East instead of moving towards the West. Because of some prior commitments, Captain Harry Manning was not able to join the crew on the journey. Paul Mantz was also not participating in the crew due to some dispute in the contract as per reports.

They started their journey on the 1st June from Oakland and travelled to Miami, Florida. From there they continued ahead with a lot of publicity and fanfare. They flew towards Central and South America and then turned towards Africa.

From there they crossed the Indian Ocean and reached

Lae, New Guinea on 29th June, 1937. A journey of 22 thousand miles was completed so far. The rest of the 7 thousand mile journey was to be made over the Pacific.

While they were resting in Lae, Amelia contracted Diarrhoea which lasted a few days. When she was recovering, many changes were made to the plane, the extra fuel was put away as reserve on board and parachutes were also packed away as they were not needed while flying along the desolate and vast Pacific Ocean.

They left for their next destination, which was Howland Island. It was 2556 miles away from where they had started and was situated somewhere between Australia and Hawaii. A flat tiny bit of land 1600 feet wide, 6500 feet long, and not more than 20 feet above the waves of the ocean, Howland Island was not easy to distinguish among the similar kind of cloud shaped islands.

But Amelia and Noonan had plans to meet this challenge. They had made an intricate plan with a number of possibilities. They had planned to use celestial navigation for tracking the routes and keeping on course. They were also carrying a radio to communicate with Itasca, the U.S. Coast Guard vessel which was stationed off the Howland Island.

They also had a compass, maps and could also use the rising sun's position for making an educated guess to find their position in relation to Howland Island. Not just that, they also had an emergency backup plan in case they needed to ditch the plane in case of empty fuel tanks to give some buoyancy to the plane.

By this, they would also get some more time for getting into their raft which was inflatable to wait for relief. They had planned that after they aligned themselves with the correct latitude of Howland Island, they would start running north and south in search of the island and the smoke plume which was to be send by Itasca.

Amelia and Noonan set out on the 2nd July, 1937 from Lae at 12:30 pm in the afternoon towards Howland Island. Even though they had this strict thought-out plan with them, it didn't work out and with a lot of unfortunate events their way, it only led to grave results later in the journey.

The short wavelength radio equipment was left behind to give more room for the fuel canisters. The equipment was capable of broadcasting radio signals for farther distances. Because of the insufficient high-octane fuel quantity, Electra only carried 1000 gallons which was 50 gallons shorter than the full capacity. The crew of Electra got into trouble from the very beginning itself.

Many witnesses who took off on July 2 also reported that there were chances that the antenna of the radio got destroyed. There were also chances that Noonan was in a lot of difficulty with the celestial navigation because of the far-reaching overcast conditions.

If this was not enough, it was later discovered that the flyers were using an inaccurate map. According to the experts, it was later shown by the evidence that the charts which Earhart and Noonan were using showed Howland Island about 6 miles off from its actual position!

When Noonan and Amelia reached the supposed position of the Howland Island, they looked into their north and south track routes in search of the island. They looked for auditory signals or any kind of visuals from Itasca, but because of the problems mentioned, they couldn't.

Due to the time lag in communication, Amelia and Noonan got into a lot more trouble than they were already in. They were 5 nautical miles off the Howland Island's actual position. To give them a signal, Itasca also released its oil burners but it was all in vain. They probably didn't get the signal, or they didn't see it. The most probable situation was that they ran out of fuel and had to ditch into the ocean.

After realising that there was no more contact with

Amelia and Noonan, Itasca started an immediate search. Even after the efforts of 9 ships and 66 aircrafts, they remained a mystery.

President Franklin D Roosevelt also authorized a rescue budget of about 4 million dollars, but nothing yielded any result. On 18th July, 1937, the search was officially brought to an end. But even after that, Amalie's husband, George Putnam invested in extra search efforts.

There was still no result though. It was acknowledged in October, 1937 that there were zero chances of finding Amelia and Noonan now. Then on 5th January, 1939, Amelia was legally declared to be dead by the LA Supreme Court.

# Chapter 3: MV Joyita Crew and Passengers

Have you ever really wondered where the day might take you? One wrong bus stop, a decision to stay in or taking a sick day may sometimes spare your life. The 25 passengers on the Joyita boat thought they were taking a two day trip to Tokelau Islands. It turned out that the trip would be their last.

Joyita was a merchant boat, but, when the Wilmington Boat Works built it as a luxury boat in 1931, the 69 foot yacht became an escape haven for the movie director Roland West and his wife, Jewel Carmenille. He was the one who named it Joyita, which means "little jewel", taken from his wife's name.

Throughout the following years the boat changed many hands. During the Second World War it was acquired by the navy. The US marines used the yacht as a patrol boat, which caused heavy damage to the old ship. The navy upgraded the pipe systems, and equipment to fit their requirements.

Two years after the war was over, most of the navy equipment was removed and the boat was sold to private owners again, when it finally landed in the hands of

Katharine Luomala. She often chartered the ship to her friend, an English born seaman, living in Samoa, called Captain Thomas H. "Dusty" Miller.

Captain Miller was in charge of the 270 mile (approximately only 430 kilometers) journey over the Pacific to the Tokelau Islands. His boat should have shipped off on October 2, 1955 with the afternoon tide, but after failures of the port engine clutch, the trip was delayed for the next day. Joyita left the shore the next day, using only one engine.

It was carrying 16 crew members, 9 passengers and 4 tons of cargo. The cargo only consisted of food, medical supplies, timber, and 80 empty drums, each capable of holding 200 liters of oil. It was supposed to arrive at Fakaofo port on October 5th (schedule was from 41 hours to 2 days), but a day after, there was still no sign of the ship.

The port sent a message that Joyita was overdue. After it was confirmed that land based operators and other ships hadn't received any distress signal from the crew, a rescue mission was sent to look for the ship. The Royal New Zealand Air Force and Sunderland searched an area of 100,000 square miles, but didn't manage to find the ship or the passengers.

Five weeks later, Captain Douglas of the Tuvalu ship spotted the Joyita at north of Vanua Levu, over 600 miles away from its scheduled route. The boat was still floating, but the deck rail was flooded. There was no trace of the crew and passengers and the cargo was missing as well. The radio was tuned to 2182 kHz, the marine distress channel.

Investigation showed light damage to the ship; crashed and damaged windows on the deckhouse, as well as a smashed flying bridge. Barnacles were growing on unusual waterlines of the boat, suggesting that the ship was floating tilted for a while.

Many investigators and researchers have tried to explain the tragic incident of the Joyita ship, but with no evidence or witnesses, and after more than 50 years, there can only be theories and speculations.

One of those theories explains that the engines' cooling system had a corroded pipe, which flooded the boat. Although it was evident that the crew tried to send signals to the port officials, it was later proven that the cable between the aerial and the set was broken, thus limiting the radio range to only 2 miles. Which means that the crew tried to call for help but probably thought no one was getting their message.

The crew had only three life jackets on the boat, so some members of the crew must have ordered the passengers to get inside the tiny life boats. They waited and waited for a rescue boat that never came, and may have eventually either drowned or were killed by sharks.

The 4 tiny lifeboats were never found either, which suggests that this theory may not be correct. This is a widely supported theory even though the boat was examined and it was determined that the hull was functional, which means the boat could've gone back to Samoa safely. This should have been clear to the 16 people working as crew, but on the contrary, mattresses were found inside the engine room, pointing to the fact that the passengers were trying to prevent the ship from flooding.

The passengers' behavior was not the only bizarre happening on this Mary Celeste type of boat. The logbook of the boat was missing, as well as most navigational equipment. One of the passengers was a doctor carrying a medical bag, but all that was left in the bag was a scalpel, stethoscope, and several bloody bandages.

The boat was found with all clocks stopped at 10:25, but before you jump to a paranormal conclusion, you need to know that the boat's generator was cut of at that time of the night. Some say the bloody bandages were a result of the fight between the captain and other crew, but the theory doesn't explain what happened to the rest of the people.

And finally, the most logical explanation is that the boat was intersected by Japanese Nazi forces, or simply fishermen. Another theory says that the boat was attacked by pirates, the cargo stolen and passengers killed. Since there was no sign of the lifeboats, some people say the passengers were kidnapped and taken to the Soviet Union.

If you still believe in a paranormal incident behind the tragic event that happened on Joyita, you should know that Joyita was taken to sea twice after this incident. Because of improperly installed valves, the ship experienced mechanical problems again, which ended it's sailing career and declared it as a potential death trap.

# Chapter 4: Brandon Swanson

It's been 5 years now but Annette and Brian Swanson still keep the light at the porch lighted for their son who went missing.

The porch light's been burning since 14th May, 2008. It was the night when Annette and Brian's son, Brandon Swanson disappeared while he was driving towards his home in Marshall, Minn.

Even though they are quite sure that they are never going to see their son alive again, they still keep the light burning in the hope of finding him some day. They know that it probably isn't possible, but they still want to believe it.

Brandon was 19 years old when he disappeared. He had gone into a ditch on a gravel road while coming back home. He called home at 1.54 am in the night and asked his parents to come pick him up near Lynd which is a small town in the southwest of Marshall. He had told them that he would be walking towards the town.

Brian and Annette went together to pick up their son. Brian had been talking to his son for about 45 minutes on the way when suddenly his son said, "Oh, s..!" and then Brandon's phone went dead. Brian said that there wasn't anything after that. That was it.

In the beginning, authorities suspected that Brandon may have fallen into the Yellow Medicine River but later they started concentrating on the area around Mud Creek which was a few miles northwest from the Porter to draw the water down and to allow the dogs to do the search in the creek beds. They made plans and obtained the permits for the search. The most recent search was administered in the month of October in 2011.

Minnesota Bureau of Criminal Apprehension received seventy-five tips about Brandon after they became the lead law-enforcement agency in 2010 on this case. This was claimed by Drew Evans, the assistant superintendent for BCA. The agency received 3 tips since 1st April. The last one was just recently.

Evans assures that they are going to keep their search open till they find any clue about Brandon. They will follow each and every lead and tip they receive. They too, like everybody else, want to see Brandon return back to his home.

About five hundred volunteers which also include 34 dog handlers from 9 different states spent more than 120 days in search of Swanson. An area of 120 sq. miles has been covered in the search as claimed by the search manager,

Jeff Hasse.

Hasse claims that it has been the biggest ever search they have had in terms of the number of missions, time length and the total number of searchers involved. Jeff Hasse is the founder of Midwest Technical Rescue Training Associates which is actually a non-profit organization that teaches the technical rescue skills to the public-safety providers. He is very hopeful regarding this case and believes that eventually, something is going to come out. Waiting is the only solution for now.

Brandon Swanson graduated in the year 2007 from Marshall High School and spent one complete year studying wind energy at Minnesota West Community College in Canby.

Brandon was wearing a blue-striped polo shirt, a baggy pair of jeans, a white coloured twin's baseball cap, a black hooded sweatshirt, a sterling silver chain necklace and wire-rimmed glasses when he disappeared.

The green coloured Chevy Lumina which belonged to Brandon was found somewhere near Taunton, between Canby and Marshall, but it was nowhere around the place where he told his parents he was. His parents assumed that he probably got confused while wandering in the dark that night and lost his way.

Officials have not found any evidence that would bring some kind of foul play into the light. There is also no indication that Brandon would have staged his own disappearance. Brandon Swanson's father, Brian, claims he was very close to his son and there is no chance that he would do something like this.

Brandon's parents still hope that some evidence will eventually turn up about their son. They have searched for their child for more than 3.5 years in an extensive manner and has not got any easier with time.

# Chapter 5: Michael Negrete

On 10th December, 1999, the UCLA Community got a big shock with the mysterious disappearance of one of the students who was living on campus. Even 3 years after the incident, detectives say that there are no signs of Michael Negrete.

But the search goes on.

Michael was a freshman at UCLA, a talented musician, an unassuming teenager with good friends and good grades, living in one of the biggest campus dorms.

Then one night, after hanging out with his dorm friends, he went down the hallway towards his room to get some sleep. He was never seen again after that. He vanished.

Nobody has seen Michael since then and do not even have a clue of what happened to him and where he might have gone or how he disappeared.

Michael was 18 years old when he went missing and crime experts say that there are a number of complex factors in the search for the missing adults. In most of the cases, there are no wrongdoings. Many adults just choose to disappear on their own, by will. They look out to start a completely new life and hope to never get found. Police, in this case, may be slow in responding because there are doubts of any kind of crime committed.

Michael's mother, Mary Negrete wants everyone to know that her son is still missing. She wants the students to keep their eyes and ears open all the time. She doesn't want that what happened to her son to happen to anyone else.

A number of methods have been used to increase the awareness of his disappearance.

Since Michael's disappearance, his case has been featured on a number of TV programs like MSNBC's "Missing Persons", "Extra", "National Inquirer TV" and just recently his mother, Mary Negrete appeared on the show called, "The Montel Williams Show".

Sylvia Browne, a renowned psychic featured in the last show and during the show, told Mary that her son Michael is still alive and is living in West LA area.

The show was telecast on 26th Feb and Browne told Mary that her son is still somewhere in or around UCLA. He is in the Brentwood, Westwood area and is not dead.

After the disappearance of Michael, a number of psychics approached Mary and claimed to have knowledge of the whereabouts of his son. But Mary says that all the cases have not led her anywhere and now it is very difficult for her to believe any psychic.

Mary claimed that she doesn't believe in Psychics at all. But she chose to go there to gain publicity.

Unluckily, she failed to get the kind of coverage she wanted and she was disappointed on the fact that her son was mentioned in the show only once.

Another method that she used to gain publicity was the website called http://findmikenow.com. This site contains all the details about Michael's appearances and the night of his disappearance.

A police composite released in the month of June in year 2000 was also featured on this website. Mary asks the students to look at the police sketches of Mike and keep a lookout for him. She still believes that there has got to be at least someone close by, or someone on the campus who could know of what happened to him.

As the time passed, Mary complained that the investigation was not running at the pace it initially began with and she was losing hope for finding her son.

Joe Purcell and Bill Howell, the LA Sheriff's detectives, have worked on this investigation case from the time it changed from the case of a missing person to a case of homicide.

From the beginning of the case, they received 500 leads and none of them were of any significance in the real sense. Bill Howells claimed that they were seriously baffled by this case. They had been in partnership together and they claim to have never come across this kind of a case ever before.

Michael disappeared in the early morning of 10th December, 1999. He was a first year student at that time and spent hours playing his computer games when he returned from a party that night.

He was last seen in the morning at 4 am on the 6th floor of Dykstra Hall. Bill Howell said that there was a witness who saw a person of Michael's description walking out of the front door at around 4:35 am.

Bill Howell says that from the start of this investigation, there had been no clue of Michael being alive. In the 3 years, since the time of his disappearance, there has been no activity on his credit card, Ralph's club card or his bank accounts. All of his possessions were left in his dorm room only.

Generally, when people want to disappear of their own will, they take some of their belongings with them which they need or want. But all the possessions of Michael were left in his room.

Mary wants help from the students at UCLA. She takes their help to put up fliers. She says that she doesn't believe in what Browne says, she doesn't want to lose out on any way of finding her son.

# Chapter 6: Ray Gricar

We often say that the world is a small place. It's quite the contrary actually, when you are trying to find someone. Friends, family members and authorities have been searching for Ray Gricar for 10 years now, without any result or significant lead.

Born in Cleveland, Ohio, Gricar left his job as a prosecutor in Cuyahoga County and moved to Pennsylvania in 1980, with his wife and their adopted daughter Lara. Soon, the news of a new persecutor moving to the area spread out, so Gricar was offered a job as an assistant for the district attorney David E. Grine. 5 years later, Grine's successor didn't want to run for the elections, so Gricar took his place and won the elections with 600 votes.

From then on, Gricar was re-elected 4 times, from 1989 to 2001. He was a successful attorney, a veteran, whose fast approaching retirement was only 6 months away. He wanted to spend time with the victims, listening to them and getting inside their psyche.

He was known for his intense cross-interrogations on the stand, so lawyers often dreaded their clients to be interrogated by him. The focus and attention to detail he put on his cases made him a successful attorney, and he was known to follow the last lead until he solved a case. He rarely exchanged pleasantries with coworkers, as he was always focused on his job and the task at hand. Even so, Gricar was known for his easy charm with the ladies.

At the time of his disappearance, Gricar and his girlfriend Patty Fornicola shared her childhood home in Bellefonte. When he left work, the morning of April 15th, they talked on the phone and he told her he was coming home. He didn't show up the same night, so Fornicola called the police to inform them that Gricar had not been home since the morning.

The police sent a notice to all departments to keep an eye on Gricar's red Mini Cooper. After the night had passed and there was still no sign of Gricar or his car, the State Police sent a helicopter to inspect the roadside. Nothing was discovered until the afternoon, when the police spotted Gricar's car, parked near the Street of Shops antique mall.

His phone was locked inside and the car keys and his wallet were missing. Further investigation showed that the car smelled like cigarettes and there was ash on the passenger seat. Since Gricar didn't smoke, the police assumed that someone was in the car with him, or at least leaned in on the passenger seat.

Still, there were no signs of violence, no blood or marks, nothing out of the ordinary. Few people at the antique mall reported seeing Gricar walking in, where he came across a tall, brunette lady who is still a mystery. There was nothing romantic in the meeting, to witnesses they seemed like old acquaintances meeting after a long time.

The police had hardly any evidence to work with, until they found out that Gricar had his laptop with him that Friday at work. They didn't find his laptop in the car or home, but the investigation showed that his home computer was used to search the internet for tips and ways on how to destroy a computer hard drive, prior to his disappearance. His computer was accidentally found in July 2005, with its hard drive missing.

They found the hard drive after two months in the upstream, around 100 yards away from the laptop. This piece of evidence was the last hope for the police, as it was believed to hold heavy information about the case. It turned out that the sand and grit damaged the drive beyond repair or functionality.

After several weeks of searching the nearby Susquehanna River with the help of curious citizens, policemen, boats and divers, the police and FBI were once again on the same track, with many theories and no real clues.

Gricar's nephew, Tony Gricar, told the police that the scene where they found his uncle's car and laptop seemed very familiar and resembled the circumstances around his father's death, Ray's brother. The court proclaimed his death to be a suicide, but his entire family never believed this story. Gricar argued at the time that his brother would never leave two sons without a father. He also said that suicide victims complete their acts in public, where there are a lot of people watching, whereas his brother's murder resembled a typical homicide scene.

The FBI peeked inside Gricar's life back to his younger days. They found that he'd been visiting Slovenia in the 70's and 80's, since it was his ancestral country. They kept track of his credit cards, bank account and cell phone records, but nothing revealed any clues about where he might have been.

When the police started suspecting that Gricar might have walked away from his old life, fliers were distributed in Slovenia to help the investigation. The audience at the Oprah Show was also introduced to the case, with hope that some of them might help the police get new leads. The police chased more than 300 reported missing persons sights resembling Gricar, from North Carolina to Arizona. At the request of his daughter, he was declared legally dead on July 25th, 2011.

One day later, the authorities in Utah were taking fingerprints of a prisoner charged with a misdemeanor. The man was around his late 60's or early 70's, just like Gricar at the time, with the same height and appearance. His fingerprints however, didn't match anyone else's in the database, and he didn't want to tell the police his real name. It was decided that the man was not Gricar, so the police continued the search.

Several graves have been dug up with no success. To end the case with another fail, the FBI hired a psychic to help them with leads. Nothing the psychic said matched the case, except when she saw a construction worker leaning on the car and talking to Gricar. The police believed that may be the reason why they'd found ashes on the passenger seat.

After that, the investigation slowed down. The police stood behind two major theories: suicide or homicide. The third theory was voluntary walk away, but it was soon discarded because Gricar had been building money in his bank account and he was months away from a safe pension. People often pointed out to his reputation of being a lady's man, suggesting that he'd found another woman who could take care of him, but his friends and family say he wasn't the type of guy who would leave his bank account and disappear, only to be with a woman.

Something has to be really going against you, for you to leave your life, your position in society and loved ones just to start a new life. The hard drive of the computer is still in the evidence room, with the hope that someday technology will advance to the point where the police can inspect what was on it. There had to be something intriguing in it, to force Cricar to break open the computer and throw its hard disk hundreds of miles away. Or was it someone else who broke the computer?

Gricar's job carried a lot of responsibility. Over the course of his 35 years as a prosecutor and then a DA, he had helped in the imprisonment of many murderers and sex offenders. Years after the investigation was over, a former Hell's Angels officer decided to contact the authorities with info about Gricar's death.

He said that a fellow Hell's Angels member went after Gricar because thanks to him, he'd received a long prison sentence in the 90's, about an aggravated assault. The informant was questioned by both the local police and the FBI. He even took them to a location in Pennsylvania, where, according to him, Gricar's body was disposed of. At the last minute he changed his mind, telling the FBI agents that there were 4 other bodies in there, as well as guns. He only told them that the murderer spun Gricar's knee caps and slit his throat.

Another homicide theory revolves around Jerry Sandusky. He was convicted of child abuse in 2011, but back in the 90's the first victim approached Gricar with accusations against the Penn State defensive coordinator. Gricar didn't press charges at the time, citing that there wasn't enough evidence against Sandusky.

There are those people, including an employee at the ice cream parlor, just across the courthouse who believed that the DA had entered a witness protection program and would re-appear after the long investigation on the mob. Many other people believe that he may have come across some evidence about the mob that governs over Pennsylvania, was threatened and disappeared to save his life and keep his family alive. Others believed he was threatened by the Sandusky people to lay off about the sexual accusations.

We may never know where Gricar disappeared. As the FBI says, killers always brag about their misdemeanors, so if someone really killed the DA, sooner or later someone will spill the beans.

# Chapter 7: Madeleine McCann

On the night of April 28th, nobody knew that a little girl called Madeleine McCann would be the head news on every television and newspaper just six days later. Madeleine, her brother and sister together with their parents, Kate and Gerry wanted to spend a wonderful spring break at the Praia da Luz, in Portugal. They went with their friends and their children and the vacation was dreamlike, until the evening of May 3, when Madeleine was abducted.

The McCanns had dinner every night with their friends at the Tapas restaurant. Earlier that day their friends reserved a table next to the pool, with a note to the staff to reserve that table and that their children were asleep in their apartments.

Kate McCann believed that the kidnapper might have read this note and acted upon it. They locked the front door, overlooking the street, but they left their patio door unlocked, to let their friends check on their kids during their routes.

The friends got together at 8:30 and at around 9:05, Madeleine's father went to check their children. He saw they were sleeping, so he went back to his table. Her mother wanted to check them again at 21:30, but one of their friends, Matthew Oldfield offered to check the McCann kids together with his own.

The kids had appeared to be sleeping, so he reported back to Kate that Madeleine and her twin siblings were sleeping. She went into the apartment to check them again at 10:00, only to discover that her daughter was missing.

When the police did the research, the McCann family got into real trouble. At the beginning of the investigation, it was discovered that the McCanns gave their kids sleeping pills. Even though they were both doctors, the persecution believed that they had killed their own daughter, by overdosing her with sleeping pills.

That was why they called the police nearly an hour after they discovered that Madeleine was gone. Later, this accusation was withdrawn, but the McCann couple were still a suspect. Matthew Oldfield was another suspect, because he was the last one to see the girl in the apartment. The police accused him of handing the girl over the window, because as the mother said, she found the window and shutters open.

Their friend Jane Tanner reported seeing a man with a child. The man was over 5 feet tall, with a Mediterranean appearance, while the child was cuffed at the feet and had light pink pajamas with floral patterns. The police didn't believe this story, because Jane said she saw Madeleine's father talking to a man on his way from their apartment to the table. The street where she passed them was very narrow, but they both said they didn't see her, which led the police to believe that Jane thought up the sight in her mind.

Another similar sight was reported by Mary and Martin Smith. They said they saw a man who seemed uncomfortable carrying the child, who had light colored pajamas, blonde hair and a pale tan. They described the man as over 5 feet tall, dark, short hair, normal build and around 30 years old. He was wearing light beige or cream trousers, and according to the Smiths, he seemed like a local.

Other witnesses saw two blond men in the apartment two doors down from the McCanns. Another blonde man was seen near the McCann apartment two hours after the first sight. The same or another blonde man was seen later, at 18:00 standing on the staircase in front of their block, and two blond men were seen again around 23:00 on the street across the McCann apartment block, speaking in raised voices. When they realized that they had been noticed, they became quiet and walked away.

A blonde man was seen on April 29th, and again on May 2nd around the McCanns apartment. The witness described him as ugly, with a large nose and pitted skin. The girl whose grandparents used to own the place where Madeleine's family was staying, described this ugly man best. She said he was in his mid-30's, Caucasian, with spots on his face, wearing a light T-shirt, a leather jacket , jeans and sunglasses.

Other witnesses reported seeing two men with dark hair, visiting the apartments near the McCann's place the afternoon of the abduction. They were collecting money for orphanages. Another witness saw a man trying to close a gate leading away from the apartment blocks, quietly and with two hands, while looking around suspiciously. One of the witnesses described him in detail. He had dark hair, large teeth and a moustache, around 40 years old and a sallow complexion.

Three of the seven friends of the McCanns said they saw Robert Murat near the resort at the evening of the kidnapping. Robert was a British local, working as a property consultant, living with his mother 150 yards away from the resort. Both he and his mother said he never left his place at the night of the abduction. The press told the police that Robert was asking about the case, which made the police suspect that he might have something to do with the kidnapping.

The police treated the McCanns as suspects mainly because they made a mockery of the investigation. As the police stated, they turned the case into a media circus. The police on the other hand, were accused by the McCanns that they were not doing their best to solve the case. At the beginning, the parents were furious because according to them, the police arrived an hour after they reported the abduction.

According to the police report, the case was reported at 22:45, the police arrived at 23:10. Patrol dogs were with the police at 2am, search and rescue dogs arrived at 8 am. All police officers left after hours, searching caves, waterways, wells, ruins and sewers. The biggest mistake the police made was not securing the crime scene right away. Tape was placed around the kid's bedroom at 3 am, but after the officer left, around 20 people entered the room.

An officer was seen dusting the window for prints without gloves or any protection, which made the McCanns suspect the quality of the Portuguese police. Border and marine police were given photos or a description of Madeleine several hours after the abduction, and according to the parents, the police failed to make detailed door to door investigations. Interpol took five days to issue a missing person report, and the companies that monitored the roadways were not approached for surveillance tapes.

The police found many inconsistencies in the interviews conducted with the McCanns as well as their friends. Their friend, Matthew Oldfield changed his statement three times. The McCann couple also, couldn't remember whether they entered the apartment from the front door or patio door. They couldn't remember whether they closed the bedroom window and its shutters or not.

Gerry said he lowered the shutter from the bedroom and went outside, where he discovered that it could be raised from the outside too. Later, it was established that once the shutter was lowered, the pulling strap was locked from the box on the inside. The shutter couldn't have been lowered from the outside unless, by using force, which there was no evidence of.

Their statements varied greatly on the 4th of May, ten days later, and at the court. The McCann couple and their friends said the variations happened during the translation, because the interviewer was Portuguese, so he asked the questions in Portuguese, while they answered in English. The interviews were not taped, only written down by an officer.

The media accused the couple and their friends of being a swingers group, sworn to secrecy about what happened that night. Disappointed by the Portuguese police, the couple hired several private investigators. They had to raise money to pay the search, but the media revealed soon after that they had paid off their mortgage of 1 million pounds with the money raised for finding Madeleine.

The public was furious, and soon rumors started to spread out about the couple's involvement in the kidnapping. Researchers and journalists, backed by the police started investigating closer and tried to link some evidence together to make a point. They started with Madeleine's mother yelling: "They have taken her."

This brought suspicion first, because Kate's first reaction seemed like she was trying to set the course toward kidnapping from the very beginning. The theory suggests that the parents might have killed Madeleine with sedatives, and then tried to make it look like a kidnapping. They hid the body for three weeks, until they found an untraceable car that could help them get rid of their daughter's body.

This was the theory that stuck for a while, until someone found a private blog with pictures of an American girl who looked just like Madeleine, named Maddy. Maddy's mother was a professional photographer and her father was a policeman. All the photos from Madeleine's posters and internet alerts were gathered, to see if there was any resemblance to the girl in America.

There was a photo of Madeleine holding tennis balls, where she had two visible bruises on both her legs. The American girl, Maddy had the same bruises on the same place. A computer program was used to investigate the photo details, and it turned out that the photo was taken just a day after the abduction of Madeleine.

Another photo of Madeleine with her father and sister at the swimming pool, showed she had a hair bead, just like Maddy had in the same place in her hair, in a photo taken two weeks later. Several photos showed similarities between the two girls, not just in their appearance but in their hobbies, clothes, etc. Almost all Madeleine's photos were tampered with. It was later questioned if she even had Coloboma, because in almost all photos the dark spot in her iris was gone, which led many to believe that the family invented the condition. They even refused to give the medical history to the police.

The photos revealed many hidden clues, which raised a suspicion that Madeleine's parents knew exactly where she was. That was why they might have given her sedatives, to keep her calm until she entered her new home. Or maybe she knew the people who were taking her, which was why none of the witnesses heard a child screaming that night. Most interestingly, the first vacation the McCann family took after the abduction was in the United States.

Many lives have been ruined after the unfortunate night of Madeleine's disappearance. Leading suspects have been under police loupe for years, while the media have been tossing innocent names around like it's a game. None of the investigators found out what really happened to the little blonde girl, though many secretly hope that the parents know where she is. Not just for closure, but because the other scenarios are far more monstrous.

# Chapter 8: Ludwig Leichhardt

Ludwig Leichhardt (Friedrich Wilhelm Ludwig Leichhardt) was born on October 23, 1813 in a village of Trebatsch which today is part of Tauche, Branderburg as the sixth child of Christian Hieronymus Matthias Leichhardt and Charlotte Sophie. He was the 4th son of a royal inspector and farmer.

Although Leichhardt did not have a professional degree, he studied natural sciences, language and philosophy midst 1831 and 1837. He did some field work in Italy, Switzerland and France while studying natural sciences in Jardin des Pnates & the British Museum when he first came to England in 1837. He called himself a doctor though.

Leichhardt traveled to Sydney, Australia in 1842 to explore inland parts of the mighty continent and moved over to the northern part of Sydney – The Hunter River Valley to study its farming methods, fauna & geology. He also visited parts of Queensland from New South Wales to collect more specimens.

With no support from the government; he along with 4 of his European friends assisted with some private funding left Sydney in August 1844, to reach Moreton Bay. The October month gave a kick start to his expedition which consisted an overland journey of 4,800 kilometers and a vast distance of sea sailing too.

The hero was welcomed graciously in March, 1846 upon his return without John Gilbert though; one of his fellow expeditors, post which he penned down the entire journey in his journal - Journal of an Overland Expedition in Australia, from Moreton Bay to Port Essington, a Distance of Upwards of 3000 km, During the Years 1844 and 1845.

With sufficient government grant and private funds again, he began his second expedition in December, 1846 which did not practically succeed and the troupe were forced back to their starting point after being subjected to bad weather conditions and minor ailments after covering 800 kms.

The annual award of Paris Geographical society was shared by Leichhardt with a French explorer Rochet d'Hericourt for his geographic discovery. In recognition to the increased knowledge of the great continent of Australia, he was the Patron's medal by the Royal Geographical Society.

With a couple of aboriginal guides - Wommai and Billy Bombat who joined the group of 5 (Leichhardt, Adolph

Classen, Arthur Hentig, Donald Stuart and Kelly) in Port Stephens; the troupe started their new expedition from Condomin river to Swan river. It was expected to last for 2-3 years.

They were helped with 50 bullocks, 7 horses and 20 mules. Speculated to be last seen in the mainland at McPherson's Station, Coogoon on 3rd April, 1848.

What happened after that remains a mystery. It was a suspicion that he would have reached Great Sandy Desert in the centre of Australia and would have disappeared after that. When no news was heard even for 4 years, he was assumed to be dead along with his fellow mates.

Some very interesting speculations produced a maze of theories in numerous ways. Where some said that the party may have been murdered; some exclaimed an aboriginal tribe as his company in far deserts. The speculations widened from the suspicion of mutiny to drowning of the entire group.

The troupe might have starved to death or Leichhardt may have been eaten by sharks in the Gulf of Carpentaria. No one knew the truth or was nearer to that until search operations did their part.

The Government of New South Wales expedited many search operations. One such expedition was headed in

1852 under Hovenden Hely with a few members who succeeded to find a tree marked "L" over "XVA". In 1858, the second operation carried out under Augustus Gregory could find two trees marked with "L" over it in approximate vicinity.

Duncan McIntyre informed the Royal society about the "L" marked over a couple of trees near the Gulf of Carpentaria in 1864. He was directed to expedite a search operation under him in December but the search produced no results either.

An expedition was soon trouped in 1869 under the supervision of John Forrest as directed by the Government of Western Australia when they heard rumors about a place where remains of horses and men killed by indigenous Australians were found. This too produced zero results. And in 1896, David Carnegie started an expedition of his own through the Great Sandy Deserts and Gibson. He found a small brass plate with Leichhard's name written over it.

Till now, there was speculation on the route Leichhardt would have taken and the distance he would have covered prior to perishing. A crucial break in 1900 lead to attain more evidence.

In 1900, a tiny 15 cm x 2 cm brass plate marked

"LUDWIG LEICHHARDT 1848" was found within the Northern Territory just inside Western Australia by an Aboriginal stockman near Sturt Creek. This place lies between Great Sandy deserts and Tanami. This plate was authenticated by Australian historians and scientists.

A national museum in Australia now owns the plate which was found attached to a boab tree with a partially burnt shotgun mark. The tree was engraved with the initial "L". The plate was examined extensively by the museum.

An intensive scan through an electron microscope by Dr Ian MacLeod of the Western Australian Museum produced evidence about the plate: Firstly, the brass was from the early 1800s. Secondly, the zinc chloride over the plate shows that it was long buried in the arid lands. And thirdly, the Sulphur residues over it lately matched the gunpowder used in that era in firearms.

The location of the brass plate however confirmed that at least two thirds of the way in his east-west crossing attempt was covered. Also, it was confirmed that he was following the northern arc following the headwaters of Mortean Bay to the Swan River in Western Australia.

The NSW State Library later produced a letter by a librarian in 2003. This letter, dated April 2, 1874 was received by William Bran white Clarke, a Sydney clergyman and was written by W.P. Gordon.

Gordon being a station owner at Darling Downs, met Leichhardt during the days when the party, according to theories, vanished. The letter contained stories by Gordon who detailed his meeting with the Wallumbilla tribe. One of those stories detailed the death of a white man heading a herd of bullocks and mules a few years earlier along the Maranoa River.

A book, 'Where is Dr Leichhardt?'was published lately on the disappearance mystery by Dr Darrell Lewis. Lewis is an archaeologist, historian and bushman who along with five Europeans and two Aboriginal guides traversed the far desert regions to find Leichhardt.

Evidence and speculations have given diverse results. Findings on this case have at the end failed to solve one of the biggest mysteries of mankind. The loss of Leichhardt remains to be one of the greatest mysteries and he himself perhaps owes us to sort the entire story.

# Chapter 9: Rebecca Coriam

Sometimes a plan to travel to exotic places may just end up in disaster. Such is the case of the young Rebecca Coriam. She was a 24 year old girl from Chester, England, always cheerful and optimistic. In her youth, she worked at the Chester Zoo, like many of her relatives. In her teens, she became a British Army cadet, where later, she secured a position as a staff volunteer. After an interview with the Disney Cruise line in 2010, she got hired at the company's theme park. Rebecca sailed off to the Bahamas, after her training in Florida.

When this arrangement ended, she had two months off, which she spent at home, in Britain. She continued working on the Disney Wonder ship as a youth worker, visiting the Mexican Riviera and the Panama Canal. During this time, her grandfather died, so she went back to Britain to be with her family. It was the last time her family saw her in person.

The case of Rebecca is still a mystery to this day. The last time her parents talked to her was on the 21st of March, 2011. She said she'd call them again the next day. Her mother started worrying when she didn't reply to her message in 12 hours. When they were getting ready for bed that night, an official from the Disney Company called to tell them that their daughter had gone missing.

Somewhere around Puerto Vallarta and Cabo San Lucas, Rebecca disappeared. She missed her shift that day, and failed to respond to the public address system the ship provided. None of her coworkers had seen her since the night before.

The ship was searched by her fellow crew members, but no sign of her was found anywhere. The officials made a call to the Mexican navy and the US coast guard, to order them to search the international waters where Wonder sailed from the night before onwards. The Disney Wonder was registered in the Bahamas, so three days after Rebecca disappeared, a detective from the Royal Bahamian Police Force was sent to investigate the case.

Apparently, he had scheduled a full week for investigating the case of missing Rebecca, but when the parents of Rebecca arrived, they found out that he only investigated the case one day, one day of which he only questioned a few crew members and no passengers at all.

When Rebecca's parents, Annmaria and Mike were flown on board from England, they were tired and hungry, so they left the hard questions for the next day. They were told that Rebecca must have been around the crew pool when a wave hit her and washed her overboard. This theory didn't seem likely to the Coriams because the walls around it were too high.

The next day they realized that the Bahamian detective had left, with so many questions unanswered. The only place where Rebecca could've slipped and fell was on Deck 4, where the railings were low enough for accidents of that kind to happen. Jon Ronson of the Guardian believed she must have jogged there on the tracks, when she slipped and fell off the deck or was washed away.

He noticed hidden cameras on the deck disguised as some sort of nautical equipment, in the form of long tubes. The ship refused to reveal the footage recorded from those cameras, apparently for safety reasons. A few of the crew-members had the courage to tell Ronson that Disney knew how the girl disappeared because every inch of the ship was under surveillance.

Only one security camera was reviewed and it showed that Rebecca was on the crew deck at 5:45am. She was talking on the internal phone with someone and she seemed distressed. A young man approached her, asking her if she was alright, to which her lips clearly move to "yeah, fine". Then she hung up the phone and put her hands in her back pockets and pushed her hair backwards.

Rebecca's family responded that, that was her typical body language. That's about the only information the company provided around the disappearing of Rebecca. The only evidence was a slipper, which everyone who knew her said it wasn't hers.

Many theories circle this mysterious case, all of which may eventually turn out to be true, if the FBI reveals what they have on the case. According to a crew member who knew Rebecca, she was involved in a love triangle. The relationship was great at first, but then it turned ugly.

Her parents, a year after her disappearance approached the man and woman they heard were involved with Rebecca. They told them that the Disney officials sent a video footage to the FBI, but the Bureau hadn't shared any details yet.

Somewhere along the line it was suggested that Rebecca might have committed suicide, judging by her emotional state on the camera records and the fact that she was involved with a man who had another woman. The family disregarded this theory because Rebecca didn't fit the profile of a suicide victim. On the ship they found out that she was planning to surprise them with tickets to Disneyland in Paris, which was something a suicidal person wouldn't do.

The woman she spoke to on the phone said she was indeed upset at the beginning, but calmed down and said she was going to her room. If she really was upset, she might have climbed on the wall to sit and relax, which ultimately ended tragically.

Even so, her parents never gave up. They still believe that she may have been washed ashore, or may have swum to the shore. She was in great physical condition and used to compete in triathlons. Their hopes sparked up again when the bank called them after they got back to England. Apparently someone had been trying to access Rebecca's account, on April 19th, which meant that she could be alive somewhere.

Since Rebecca disappeared, her parents have not received any update about the case. The officials from Disney, as well as the police in the Bahamas tell them that the investigation is ongoing.

Stephen Mosley is the MP for Chester, who criticized both the Disney company and the Bahamian police forces. According to him, the company is more concerned to see their ships sailing smoothly, than solving cases where their own crew was involved. Rebecca was not the only case of a missing person, although she is the first one on the Disney Wonder.

Ever since, nothing has changed after Rebecca's disappearance, without news about any clues or sightings. No amount of pressure seems to be enough for the responsible people to step up and finally solve the case. The family is left hoping that their daughter may have lost her memory during the potential fall.

# Chapter 10: Helen Brach

In a twist of fate, the multimillionaire widow Helen Brach who lived her life in luxury and her supreme bred horses, disappeared and died because of those two very two things. Helen was 65 when she disappeared from Rochester, Minnesota.

Though Helen was not really born in the best of circumstances and she didn't have much growing up, she left town when she got divorced at 21 and met millionaire Frank Brach at a country club in Palm Beach. They got married almost a few weeks after meeting, they had two children together and were very happy. But as luck would have it, Frank died leaving all his fortune to his wife which made her a multimillionaire.

On 17th February 1977, the day of her disappearance, Brach had left from Mayo Clinic in Rochester, Minnesota to catch a flight to her Chicago mansion. But, she never made it to the airport.

An employee of a gift shop just near the clinic had claimed to have heard that Brach was waiting for her houseman. And according to the statements given by the crew of the commercial airline, Brach was supposed to travel through but she did not make it to the flight. They were pretty certain about this fact because with a stature and special carriage like Brach, it was pretty hard to not notice her.

Though her houseman and chauffeur, Jack Matlick gave a completely different story. He claimed to have received Brach at the O'Hare airport. This made no sense at all to the authorities because during this time Brach had made no contact over the phone with anyone, which was too weird to be true for a telephone addict like Brach. And Matlick had also added that she was dropped at the airport without any luggage and three hours early.

The houseman came under suspicion by the police because of a lot more reasons than just his confusing and varying statements - He had cashed out cheques that were written by Brach, he had a room of Brach's Chicago mansion completely re-carpeted and repainted in the claimed four day period and he actually waited two weeks to report his employer as missing.

In fact, he also failed a lie detector test that was put out by the authorities. And later, he also had to surrender his share in Brach's estate because he was threatened for legal action to be taken against him for stealing $100,000 worth of gold coins from Brach's Chicago home.

Though Matlick was always the main suspect in the case, the authorities soon had to give up on this theory because there was no solid evidence found against him. Maybe it was because he destroyed all the evidence in repainting and renovating that one room in Brach's mansion, but maybe we will never know. Brach's brother also believed that Matlick was the one responsible for her sister's murder but Matlick always denied any involvement in the case. Matlick died in 2011 in a nursing home in Pennsylvania.

Another theory put forward was Richard Bailey's involvement in the disappearance of Brach. Helen had met Bailey in 1973 and by 1975 they were in a relationship and completely inseparable. Bailey was thought of using Brach just for her money and nothing else.

According to a case filed against Bailey in a different court, he was a conman who targeted middle aged or older women with little or no knowledge about horses who had recently been widowed or divorced. He had a very well built screening processes for these women.

First he courted them, flirted with them and took them to expensive restaurants and if at any point he realised the woman was not as wealthy as he thought, he would stop meeting them.

In one of his ploys, he would claim to be falling short of cash temporarily and let the victim know that he had found an amazing horse which would prove to be a great investment in order to convince the victim to shell out money. Then, he would use that horse as collateral to get a loan from the victim which is obviously never repaid.

Making the victim the owner of the horse also meant the victim was supposed to pay all the boarding bills of the horse, the non-payment of which meant Bailey had the opportunity to take back the horse.

Another one of his ploys was to try and buy a horse by involving the seller. He would usually tell the victim that he had found a great horse but it was quite expensive and then convinced the victim to buy the horse in a joint partnership with him, while Bailey would already settle a price with the seller beforehand.

When he went to see the horse with the victim, he would bargain down to a price already discussed with the seller, both Bailey and the victim would make out same price cheques to buy the horse. But only the victim's cheque was cashed and divided equally between the seller and Bailey.

Brach being an animal lover had a lot of dogs and horses, in fact she loved getting newer and better horse breeds whenever she got the chance, and Bailey took advantage of it.

It was stated that Bailey's brother Paul had sold 3 horses worth $20,000 at a price of $98,000 to Brach. And not just that, it was also claimed that Brach bought a group of very expensive brooded mares. By 1977, Brach started realizing that Bailey was only trying to rip her off. When Bailey arranged a big expensive showing for Brach in a hope that she would invest at least $150,000 in horses, she abruptly left the showing in half an hour.

Brach hired an appraiser who told her that she had invested absolutely nothing in training one of her horses, while Bailey had claimed to have hired a trainer who took $50,000. Around the same time, Brach had confided in a friend and told her she was very disturbed about her recent horse purchases from a man. She had decided to go to the State Prosecutor after returning from her visit from the Mayo clinic in Rochester but sadly she never made it.

Though Bailey could not be convicted for Brach's murder, because of the lack of evidence against him. The new evidence that turned up in 1989 with the help of the associates of Bailey, he was convicted of conspiring and defrauding Brach. Bailey was given a life sentence.

People still believe that because Bailey was convicted, he was the one who murdered Brach, but then what about the houseman Matlick who had a lot of evidence going against him? If he didn't kill Brach, why would he take two weeks to report that she had gone missing and in those two weeks completely renovate a room of her home? There are too many coincidences here to be avoided.

And no one still knows where her body actually rests. But her parents decided to put up a stone to always remember her. A marble monument in memory of Helen Brach lies in Hopedale. Her two dogs Candy and Sugar are buried right next to her.

# Chapter 11: Lieutenant Felix Moncla - Kinross Incident

The universe is a huge place, so saying there isn't life outside the earth could potentially be misleading. The Kinross incident proves that there might be someone out there, with equipment and technology a little more sophisticated and updated than ours.

According to the official records, the weather on the 23th of November in 1953 was stable. Some light clouds here and there, snow outbreaks every now and then, and absolutely no turbulences. Maybe the steady earth air attracted, what the operators described as a spacecraft.

The night was pretty uneventful at the Air Defense Command Ground in Sault Ste, until the operators detected an unidentified target over Lake Superior on their radars. The Kinross Air Force Base was the closest base to the scene, where the 433d Weapons Squadron was alerted and an all-weather interceptor was rushed out of the base.

First Lieutenant Moncla and Second Lieutenant Robert L. Wilson had the duty to inspect what the unknown object on the radar was. Wilson was acting as the interceptor's radar operator, but since the target was moving he had trouble tracking it. Ground radar operators stationed at the Keweenaw Peninsula helped the two pilots in the air by giving them directions towards the unidentified object.

Their teamwork paid off, because soon, Moncla closed in on the object. The operators watched how the two blips seemed to have merged on the radar screen, so they naturally thought that Moncla must have flown over or under the object. Moments later, the Identification Friend or Foe (IFF) signal was lost, Moncla couldn't be contacted on the radio and the blip from the interceptor never appeared again.

The USAF and the RCAF both mounted a search and rescue operation, but they never found a single trace of the interceptor or the pilots.

After the US Air Force investigation, it turned out that Moncla and the object did merge, but that was expected to happen. Apparently, the other object was another aircraft, a Royal Canadian RCAF C-47 Skytrain, which had been traveling off course, so Moncla's F-89 jet was sent to investigate.

After the radio and the IFF signal loss, the USAF stood behind the statement that a pilot from another interceptor heard a radio transmission 40 minutes after the accident. The Air Force investigation said that Moncla must have experienced vertigo and crashed into the lake.

Controversies around the Kinross incident prevail to this day. The case was not even labeled as a UFO incident, but was rather investigated by air safety specialists. However, in 1961 and again in 1963, squadron leader W. B. Totman, in an interview with the National Investigation Committee on Aerial Investigation, said that their planes were not involved in such an exercise on that day. He also stated that the C-47 was flying over Canadian territory.

Since then, many UFO researchers, enthusiasts and writers have been trying to track down some sort of evidence to be able to explain what happened to the interceptor and the pilots. Parts of a military jet aircraft were found on the shore of Lake Superior in 1968, which the US Air Force said could belong to the crashed jet in 1953. The Canadian government, however, said that no records of the kind were received by them, and the identity of the parts discovered was never published.

The enigmatic story of the jet swallowed by a spacecraft was resurrected once again in 2006. A group of Michigan divers and engineers said to have found the wreckage of the F-89 and another, unknown, teardrop shaped object nearby. They called themselves Great Lakes Dive Company, with Adam Jimenez as their spokesman.

The company posted sonar imaging of what they had discovered, and were interviewed by UFO researchers and radio hosts. Shortly after, journalists and UFO investigators claimed that their discovery was a hoax because the company turned out to be non-existent and a record of their spokesman Adam Jimenez could not be found. The company's website where they shared their discoveries disappeared and Adam Jimenez could not be contacted through emails or phone.

Exactly what happened during that night still remains uncertain. The US is known for keeping UFO secrets to themselves, so we may never know how the jet and the pilots disappeared without leaving a trace.

# Chapter 12: Leah Roberts

Most missing person cases involve either vulnerable people, people unable to protect themselves or incidents out of people's control. The case of Leah Roberts from Durham, North Carolina, depicts a young free spirit, who, unlike most missing people, maybe doesn't want to be found.

Leah was 23 years old when she disappeared. Both of her parents had died in the course of a few short years, while she was still recovering from a life-threatening car accident, which ended with an operation where a metal rod was inserted in her leg to help her heal. The events left her overwhelmed, shocked and a little powerless to face the cruel reality.

She was an excellent student with a degree in Spanish and a few more credits away from earning an anthropology degree. She dropped out, a few months away from getting a complete degree, a decision often debated between her, her sister Kara and her brother Heath. She stayed behind her decision to leave school, and started frequenting local coffee places.

There, she spent her time writing poetry and journals, where she explored the meaning of life. She often made new friends, usually discussing mutual hobbies like music, photography and reading. Leah had a kitten named Bea, whom she took with her when she went on her spiritual journeys.

Jack Kerouac was her favorite writer, especially his book The Dharma Bums, in which several scenes were set where her car was found, at Desolation Peak. Leah made plans with her roommate, Nicole Bennett and a friend named Jeannine Quiller to go on a road trip and re-enact the scenes from Beat Generation, by Kerouac.

March 9, 2000 was the day when Leah talked to her sister to let her know about her future plans. Later that day, she and Nicole agreed to babysit together for the next day, after which Leah took off. After her roommate got back from her job, she noticed that Leah's white Jeep Cherokee was missing, but she continued with her day as normal, since Leah used to stay in coffee shops for long intervals of time. On March 11, Leah still wasn't back, so on March 12, her roommate reported her missing to the police.

When her roommates searched her room, they found out that a lot of her clothes were gone. They also found a note with an illustrated Cheshire cat's grin, which said that she was not suicidal, that she was the opposite. Together with the note, she left money to cover her part of the expenses and rent. She took her cat, some money and left on a spiritual journey.

After her parent's death, her older sister Kara had power of attorney over her, so she could check Leah's financial records. Kara was happy when she discovered that her sister used her debit card to check into a motel in Memphis, Tennessee and had withdrawn a few thousand dollars on the 9th of March. Later, there were records of using the card for food and gas, as well as one last record of filling the tank at a gas station in Brooks, Oregon on March 13.

When all her credit card activity ended, her sister wanted to find out why Leah took a road trip to the Pacific Northwest. Kara and Leah's roommate went to her favorite coffee shop to talk to her friend, another Dharma Bums fan. They found out that Leah was overpoweringly moved by the scenery described in the book, around the Cascade Mountains of Washington, so she probably went there to experience its beauty. Kara went home, believing her sister would call her for her birthday on March 18.

Instead of a birthday card, Kara received a note from the sheriff office to call an office in Bellingham, Washington. Apparently, a couple reported seeing clothes scattered on a road and trees nearby, near Mount Baker-Snoqualmie National Forest. The police checked the site and found Leah's jeep, severely damaged, but without her in it. Their first association was a car crash, because the jeep went down a steep embankment, going through trees and challenging bumps.

There were no blood stains, stretched seat belts or shattered glass, although the contents of the car were scattered around, which suggested that the car may have rolled over a couple of times. It almost seemed like the car was pushed down the mound. Robbery was not a possible scenario, because money and jewellery were found around the crime scene. The cat carrier was still in the car, although she must have taken the cat with her when she left.

The setting inside the car (blankets and pillows hanging on the windows) suggested that the car may have been used as a shelter for some time. The police searched the area, together with sniffing dogs but the search didn't bear much fruit.

Her brother and sister flew in immediately to help with the investigation. They took souvenirs Leah gathered from her visit. A theater ticket from American beauty was in there, from Bellis fair in Bellingham.

They figured that she must have gone to the only sit-down restaurant in the mall, where the police found two men who had talked to Leah. They talked about her road trip plans, and she left with a man she called 'Barry'.

Her friends and family became much more worried when the car was investigated. The report suggested that she may have been a victim of a crime after all. The police found it odd she spent very little money for the time she spent in the city, and their second clue was her mother's engagement ring.

People who knew her said she must have lost her mind and forgotten who she was to leave that ring behind, because she always wore it, since it was a treasured connection to her mother. Footage from a security camera at the gas station in Oregon showed Leah clear-headed and in good condition, although she often glanced at the parking lot, a place of the gas station not covered by security cameras. If there was footage of the parking lot, the police may have been able to see if the 'Barry' character really existed.

The police received several other leads after the initial investigation. A man called the police to inform them that his wife saw Leah confused and disoriented at a gas station near Seattle. The police did not get a chance to identify him because he panicked and hung up on them. Her case was aired several times on lifetime and unsolved mysteries, which resulted in several reports of alleged sightings, but none of them proved to be credible.

At last, the family contacted Monica Caison, a woman who helps missing person cases, by keeping their stories alive in the media. She followed Leah's route around the country with a caravan to raise awareness and bring her face and story again for the public to see.

One possible breakthrough in the case was when two young detectives took over the case when the appointed detective, Mark Joseph retired. They took the investigation a little further, and inspected the Jeep's hood. They found out that a wire connected to the starter solenoid was cut. When this wire is cut, the Jeep could accelerate without a person pushing the gas pedal.

This gave clearance to the theory in the initial investigation that the car wasn't driven when it went down the hill. They also discovered unknown DNA and fingerprints. When examining the case, they noticed that the man, who claimed Leah left with a man named Berry, was a mechanic with a military background.

Unfortunately, he moved to Canada, making the investigation difficult. With the help of crime TV shows, by the end of 2011 it was determined that the fingerprint did not belong to the man the detectives suspected, but they still couldn't get his DNA for testing.

# Conclusion

Thank you again for purchasing this book!

After reading the cases of the people above, you must have some of your own theories as to what really happened in their sudden disappearance. Although your theories cannot be proven, it's a nice mental exercise.

Remember these are just a few cases-- there are still a lot of missing person/s reports that are unsolved up to now. Take whatever lesson you can from this book, to prevent sudden disappearances from happening to you, or your loved ones.

If you enjoyed this book, do you think you could leave me a review on Amazon? Just search for this title and my name on Amazon to find it. Thank you so much, it is very much appreciated!

# Want more books?

Would you love books delivered straight to your inbox every week?

Free?

How about non-fiction books on all kinds of subjects?

We send out e-books to our loyal subscribers every week to download and enjoy!

All you have to do is join! It's so easy!

Just visit the link below to sign up and then wait for your books to arrive!

www.LibraryBugs.com

Enjoy :)